MASSACHUSETTS
A View from Above

Looking at Salem from above allows you to witness the richness of the architecture and landscaping created by past generations and preserved by their current caretakers.

MASSACHUSETTS
A View from Above

CHARLES FEIL

Down East Books  Camden, Maine

ISBN 0-89272-421-8
Book design by Janet Patterson
Color separations, printing, and binding by Regent Publishing Services
Printed in Hong Kong

1 3 5 4 2

Down East Books/Camden, Maine

LIBRARY OF CONGRESS CATALOGING-IN-PUBLICATION DATA

Feil, Charles, 1948-
Massachusetts, a view from above / Charles Feil.
p. cm.
ISBN 0-89272-421-8 (hardcover)
1. Massachusetts—Aerial photographs. I. Title.
F65.F48 1998
917.44'0022'2—dc21 98-35380
CIP

Dedication

To Maralyce Ferree for all her loving support.
To my son, Dylan, for his sensitive insights.

To all the general-aviation pilots,
who will truly understand what these photographs are about.

To the air-traffic controllers—especially in Portland, Maine, and Boston—
who have been my eyes in the sky all these years.
It's a great system that works!

A special thanks to the great staff at Down East Books,
who have believed in and supported this unique concept
from the beginning.

Plum Island Beach, just south of Newburyport, is sprinkled with Victorian homes and weathered sand dunes. Flying late in the afternoon afforded me a wonderful opportunity to capture the long shadows of the houses against the sawgrass and rounded mounds of sand along the beachfront.

The latest love of my life

is not a beautiful woman but *Rooty Kazooty,* a two-seat homebuilt experimental gyroplane. I found her in 1996 at the world's largest fly-in, held every August in Oshkosh, Wisconsin.

It was on my second day there that I ran into the good folks of Rotary Air Force, a family operation that has been refining the gyroplane's unique characteristics for decades. All it took was a demonstration flight, and I was digging out my wallet and shoving my credit card into their hands. With a purchase agreement safely in my clutches, I began three months of dreaming until my kit arrived.

With a lot of advice and help, I began to assemble this heap of parts into my dream flying machine. In the spring of 1997 she was test flown and deemed worthy of receiving her FAA certification and tail number (N7234U). Now, it was time to learn to dance with this fine looking lady. I was already a commercial, instrument-rated pilot in fixed-wing aircraft, but this would be a whole new way to fly.

Operating a gyroplane is something like flying a single-engine airplane without the wings. Here, the basic stick-and-rudder controls are linked to a pair of overhead rotor blades, to which you apply power using a pre-rotator control on the stick. Once the blades are spinning at about 150 rpm, you bring the control stick back into your lap, advance the throttle, let go of the pre-rotator handle, and in about fifty feet or less, you are airborne and climbing vertically into the heavens.

The advantages of the gyroplane over an airplane are extensive, particularly in my work: aerial photography. The gyro has more maneuverability, better hovering capability, and unobstructed visibility. Moreover, it will float back to earth and land within ten feet of the target with no power from the engine. It also has pitch and roll trim

Lying in the migratory path of a large number of eastern bird species, Plum Island is an ecological wonderland of marshes, sand dunes, and meandering water.

Of Plum Island's nine-mile length, fully seven miles are occupied by the Parker River Wildlife Refuge. Of necessity, then, most of the houses and shops are concentrated in one place.

controls so that you can remove your hands from the stick, and it will fly straight and level. The best part is that the gyro is inexpensive to operate—about $10.00 an hour. Compare that to a helicopter at $250 an hour or more, and it's clear why *Rooty Kazooty* is my choice as a photographic platform.

Despite her many attributes, however, the gyro is not an easy lady to dance with. Fortunately, Curtiss Patten was an exceptional instructor who instinctively understood the strengths and weaknesses in my flying. Within a couple of weeks of intensive training, he had me ready for my flight test, and I soon added another rating to my license: Rotorcraft Operations. Now I was ready to rumba with my new love.

I set out to become proficient enough that I could fly and photograph at the same time without endangering any person or thing—including myself. After many hours of practice, the machine and I became one and my photography skills and instincts lit up like a Christmas tree.

I hope you'll try to visualize me and my lady, soaring above the treetops at 500 feet, looking at shapes, light, and shadows that are transformed in my camera and presented to you in this book. I hope, too, that my images of Massachusetts grab your imagination and massage your heart as you marvel at the brilliant sculpting done by both man and Mother Nature.

Enjoy the view!

—Charles Feil

Newburyport is the last town on the Merrimac River before that waterway spills into the North Atlantic.

The stoic twin lights of Thatcher Island on Cape Ann have kept many a sailor from going aground on the treacherous rocky coastline between Gloucester and Halibut Point.

Many of the great whaling ships passed Eastern Point Lighthouse, in Gloucester, on their way to the fertile grounds of the North Atlantic.

Handsome Abbott Hall, in the foreground, overlooks Marblehead Neck.

Tinker Island and its seasonal cottages stand guard off the southern tip of Marblehead.

Marblehead Lighthouse's beacon announces to the wayward sailor that there is a safe and secure mooring in this popular summer resort town. That's the Boston skyline in the distance.

Lexington is famous for its Revolutionary War history.

Fall brings a splash of color to Concord's Walden Pond.

I think Henry David Thoreau would have enjoyed joining me in my cockpit and sharing this view of his beloved Walden Pond.

This shot contrasts the fast-moving rush hour traffic along Route 128 near Waltham with the tranquil waters of the Cambridge Reservoir.

Stately Brandeis University overlooks the banks of the Charles River in Waltham.

At the Newton Yacht Club on the Charles River, sculling skills are honed and refined in a competitive sport shared by the many universities and colleges along the banks of this famous waterway.

Harvard University, in Cambridge, is the alma mater of some of our nation's best known physicians, educators, legislators, and business leaders.

Harvard University and its athletic fields border both the Cambridge and Boston banks of the Charles River.

Sailboats mingle on the Charles River as late-afternoon commuters make their way home along Storrow Drive and the well preserved Charles River Reservation.

Bunker Hill monument, in Charlestown, is a moving memorial to those who died in one of the bloodiest battles of the Revolutionary War.

Boston, New England's largest city, is host to many of our country's best known corporations, universities, sports teams, and historical events. From above, the city presents an eclectic architectural mix of the old and new.

Fenway Park, home to the Boston Red Sox, is nestled in the community of Back Bay.

The challenge and exhilaration of simultaneously flying and photographing are captured in this image of Boston Harbor at sunset. I am communicating with air-traffic control, stabilizing my aircraft two hundred feet above the water, and composing and timing the beacon of Boston Light. What a thrill when it all comes together!

Scituate Harbor is ideally located for boating enthusiasts who want to take day trips to Boston or Gloucester, or try the bountiful fishing in Cape Cod Bay.

Set off on a finger of beachfront, Humarock seems to be an ideal community that is close to the amenities of the greater Boston area but isolated from its more populated suburbs.

The late-afternoon sun casts long shadows on this golf course, near Accord.

Lighting and design were major elements in the making of this photograph of Gurnet Point Beach near Duxbury.

One of the joys of flying along at five hundred feet is spotting the incongruous nature of the landscape. This church steeple jutting above the trees in Duxbury was one of those sights.

Myles Standish State Park with its monument is an oasis of wilderness near South Duxbury. That's the Boston skyline in the background.

Sunset illuminates the mud flats at low tide in Plymouth Bay.

Plimoth Plantation is a marvelous re-creation of the first settlement in what would become Colonial America.

Every year, thousands of tourists come to visit the replica of the *Mayflower,* where their imaginations can re-create the voyage that their ancestors made to the New World.

Between Plymouth and Buzzards Bay there are numerous cranberry bogs whose tart fruit is harvested each fall. Most companies now use the wet-harvest method, which involves flooding the fields, mechanically agitating the bushes so the berries come off and float to the surface, and "herding" the loose fruit with strings of timber, visible here to the left.

One of only a handful of fruits native to North America, cranberries thrive in wet, acidic peat soil like that found in the southeastern part of the state and Cape Cod.

Snaking its way out into Cape Cod Bay, Jeremy Point is an extended sand bar off Wellfleet.

Sagamore Highlands and the adjacent beach are located north of the Cape Cod Canal's eastern end.

Summer cottages line Pilgrim Beach, in Truro.

When I'm in the air, my camera is like the artist's brush, and my canvas is a thin layer of emulsion on acetate. Like the artist, I freeze a moment when light, texture, and shape meet as one. Race Point on the northwestern tip of Cape Cod presented me with one of those moments.

Serving as a landmark, Pilgrim Monument looms over the homes of the lively fishing village of Provincetown, originally settled by the Portuguese.

Nauset Beach stretches along the ocean side of the Cape Cod peninsula.

Cape Cod National Seashore encompasses a forty-mile stretch of the peninsula, running from Chatham to Provincetown. Established in 1961, it encompasses 43,557 acres, which are now preserved from development. This meandering marsh lies above Orleans.

The mosaic pattern of a golf course reaches to the sea along Eastward Point, North Chatham.

Only a sliver of beach separates the mighty Atlantic Ocean from these boats, which are moored in the peaceful waters of Chatham's Pleasant Bay.

A stately mansion at the southern tip of Chatham captures the romance of a moment in time revisited every summer.

Monomoy Island National Wildlife Refuge is located on the southeastern tip of Cape Cod and demonstrates the unspoiled beauty that must have characterized the entire peninsula at one time. You have to see this place from the air to truly appreciate its uniqueness.

The Audubon Society manages Tern Island Sanctuary, which lies right off Chatham (visible in the background).

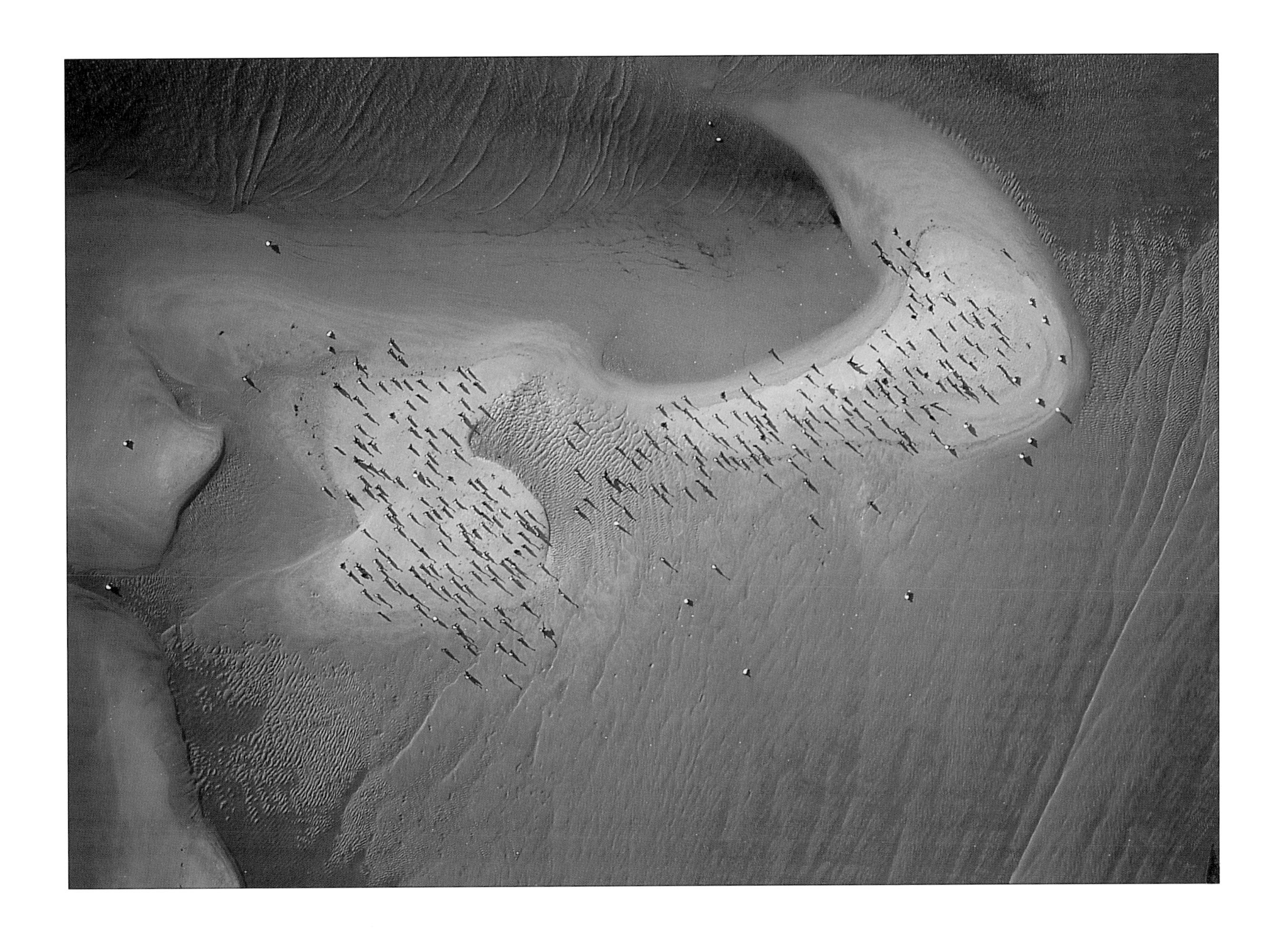

Birds congregate on an isolated sandbar just off Monomoy.

While flying over Monomoy, I was privileged to witness this gathering of seals, sunbathing without human encroachment. (I kept a higher altitude, so as not to disturb these sleeping beauties.)

Multicolored umbrellas dot a white sand beach on Nantucket's north shore.

It is a long trip in a four-wheel-drive vehicle out to Great Point, but by all accounts the journey is worthwhile if you want to watch the sun setting on Nantucket Sound. (From my vantage point in the air, I was able to appreciate both views.)

Perched at the edge of the North Atlantic is the easternmost community of Wauwinet on Nantucket Island. Here, I'm flying toward Great Point.

One of Nantucket's ferry boats passes through the fading sunset of another magnificent summer day.

A particularly long jetty demonstrates its usefulness in protecting the sailboats in the harbor at Vineyard Haven on Martha's Vineyard.

The traditional Nantucket theme of faded-shingle siding and white-gravel driveways is carried on in this condominium complex.

Gay Head prominently juts its kaleidoscopic cliffs out into the Atlantic.

The beach at Gay Head, on the western tip of Martha's Vineyard, is a popular spot for those desiring more private sunbathing. (I believe they found my overflights to be a bit of an intrusion on their ritual.)

The bright, variegated sediment of the Gay Head cliffs serve as a warning that the dangerous reef known as Devil's Bridge lurks beneath the waters below the lighthouse.

Once a thriving textile center, Fall River is nestled along the border between Massachusetts and Rhode Island.

Working schooners by the thousands once sailed the waters of Buzzards Bay. Now just a few give their passengers the experience of a fresh breeze and tight canvas.

New Bedford is home to a famous but dwindling fishing fleet that pursues species ranging from yellowtail flounder to broadbill swordfish.

The lightship *New Bedford* once greeted the city's trawlers on their return from days and even weeks of fishing off the Atlantic shelf.

Rich in maritime history, New Bedford is sprinkled with homes built by the sailors, fishermen, and fleet owners who made this city renowned.

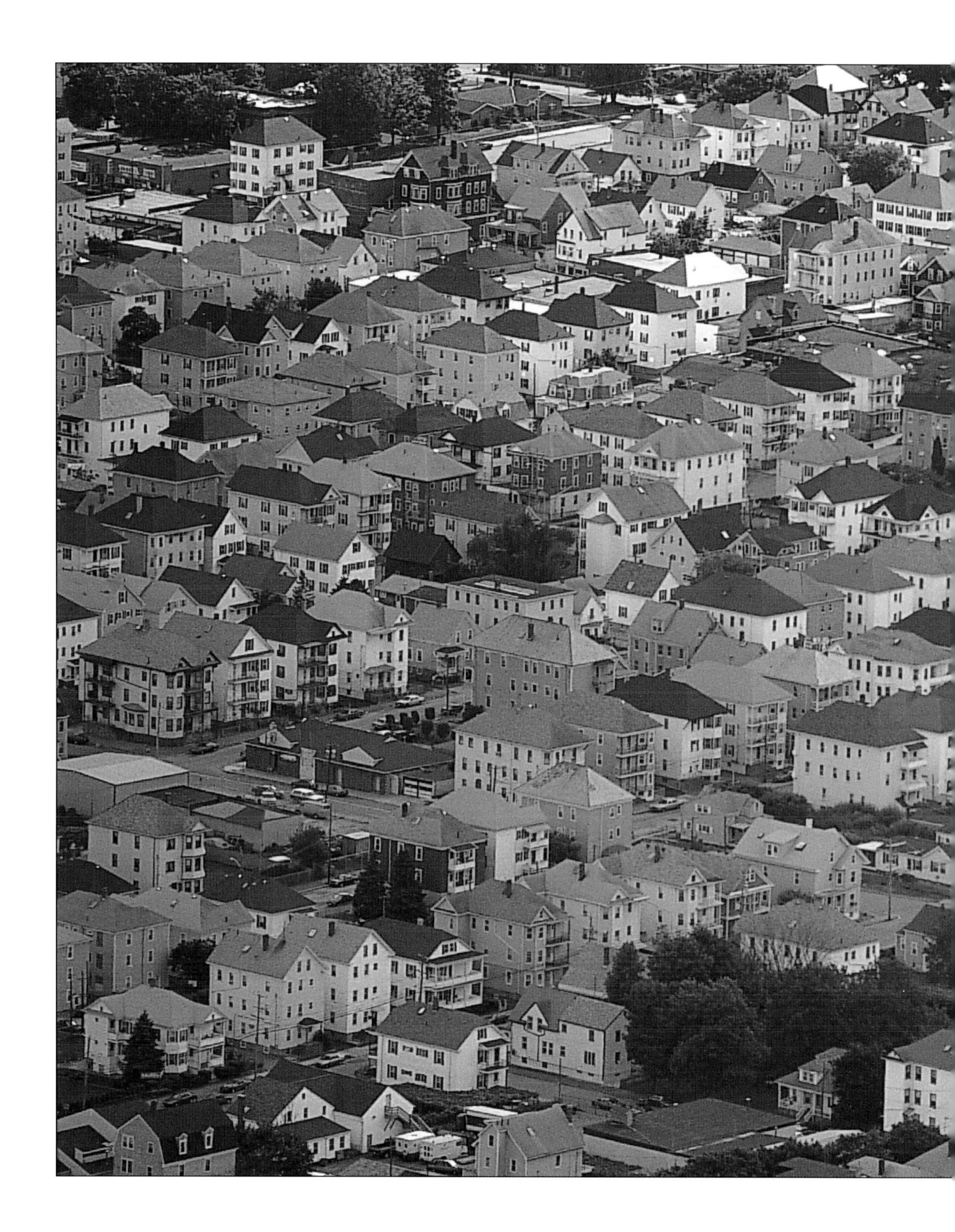

Walgreens
Walgreens
Merit

Navigable waterways that could also produce power for the mills were a key factor in the early development of textile centers like Lawrence, whose red-brick buildings have survived the ravages of fire and tough economic times.

Though Massachusetts has lost a frightening number of its farms, there are exceptions. I spotted this prosperous-looking operation near Fitchburg.

Treetop-level flying often affords me the opportunity to view sights that are invisible from ground level. This automobile salvage yard near Fitchburg was appealing in the way the wrecks had been neatly placed in rows, as if they were parked in a lot.

Interstate 290 slices a black tarmac path right through downtown Worcester.

This modern glass building in downtown Worcester reflects a later period in the city's colorful history.

Holy Cross College is just one of the highly respected educational institutions in Worcester.

Several abandoned communities lie beneath the man-made Quabbin Reservoir, which is known as the eastern boundary of western Massachusetts.

Nance Lake near New Salem seems to have gained a few extra islands over the winter.

Sunset bathes the Quabbin Reservoir in hues of purple, yellow, and blue.

Home to an armory that produced some of the most important firearms in American history, Springfield borders the Connecticut River.

The Memorial Bridge connects Springfield to its sister, West Springfield.

Traditional red-brick mills dominate the landscape in the industrial city of Holyoke, which lies along the Connecticut river between Northampton and Springfield.

The high-rise buildings of the University of Massachusetts at Amherst dwarf the traditional homes and small-town streets that surround the campus.

Smith College in Northhampton has bucked a national trend toward coeducation and continues to admit only women.

The rich farmland of Northhampton embraces the town's municipal airport.

Ashfield sits among the foothills of the famed Berkshires.

Shelburne Falls, a community of artists and craftspeople, lies along the Deerfield River.

A couple of true hairpin turns make the ride a little more interesting along Route 2, east of North Adams.

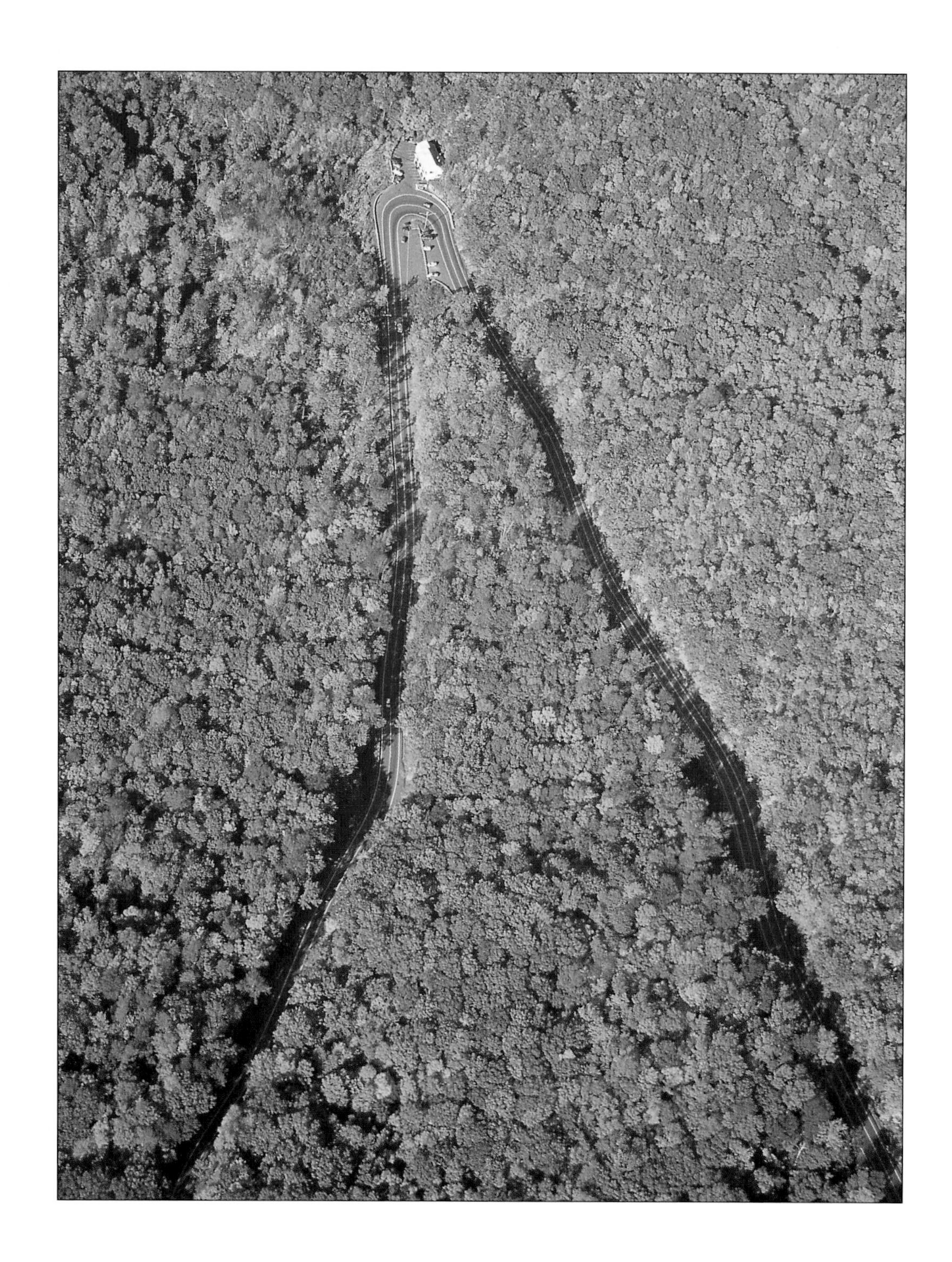

Ice and snow allow an aerial photograph to be better defined and permit improved contrast between the multiple elements of an image. This stream, running between the woods and a cornfield is a good example.

An average annual snowfall of eighty-three inches and an awesome array of snow guns make the twenty-one trails of the Bousquet Ski Area in Pittsfield some of the best in the state.

Late sun highlights the manmade striations in the rock of a North Adams quarry.

Deciduous trees in the full flush of fall meet an extensive stand of evergreens on a hillside near North Adams.

Algae coats a section of the Cheshire Reservoir south of Adams.

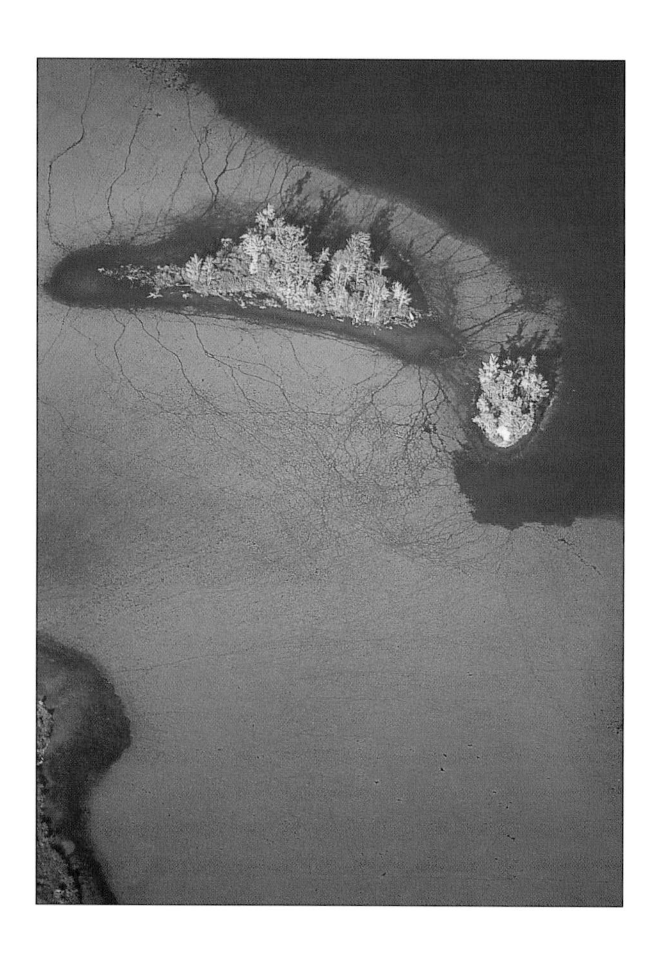

At 3,491 feet, Mount Greylock is the highest point in the state of Massachusetts.

Ice forms myriad patterns on Lower Bear Swamp Reservoir, near Ashfield.

Upper Bear Swamp Reservoir looks strangely out of place among the rounded foothills of the Berkshires.

I had to make several passes in my flying machine before successfully capturing the altitude of Upper Bear Swamp Reservoir.

A hillside of colorful hardwood trees slopes down to a pond outside North Adams.

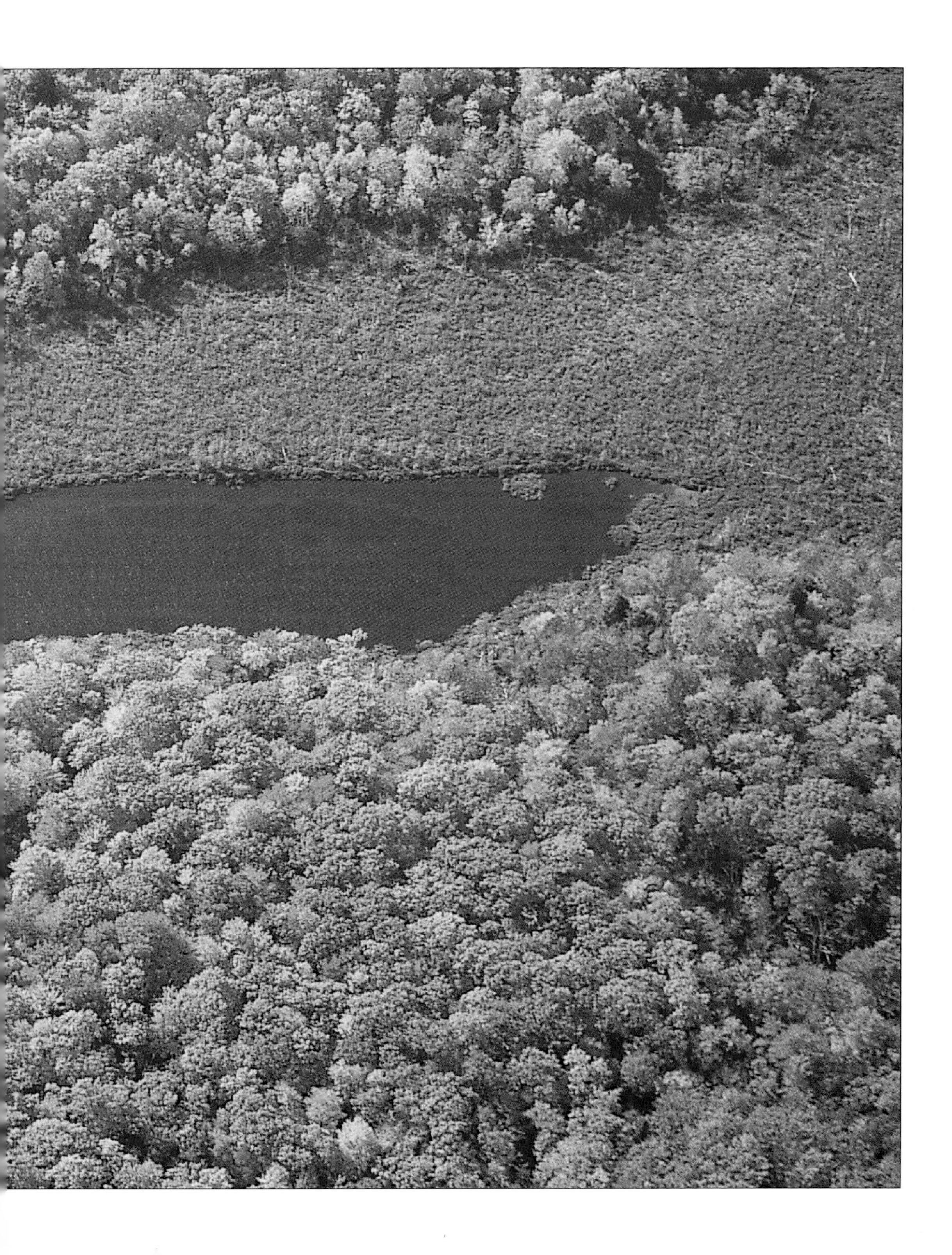

Fall foliage surrounds a lake in western Massachusetts, near Lenox.

Fall foliage and harvested fields create a mosaic on this landscape near Lenox, home of the famous Tanglewood Summer Music Festival.

Geometrically aligned cemetery plots near Lenox are framed by autumn colors.

Snow and late-afternoon sun added the depth needed to enliven this winter scene.

Colorful trees mingle in a once-soggy bog in the Housatonic area.

A silent army of denuded hardwood trees surrounds a handful of evergreen holdouts in the snow-covered western hills.

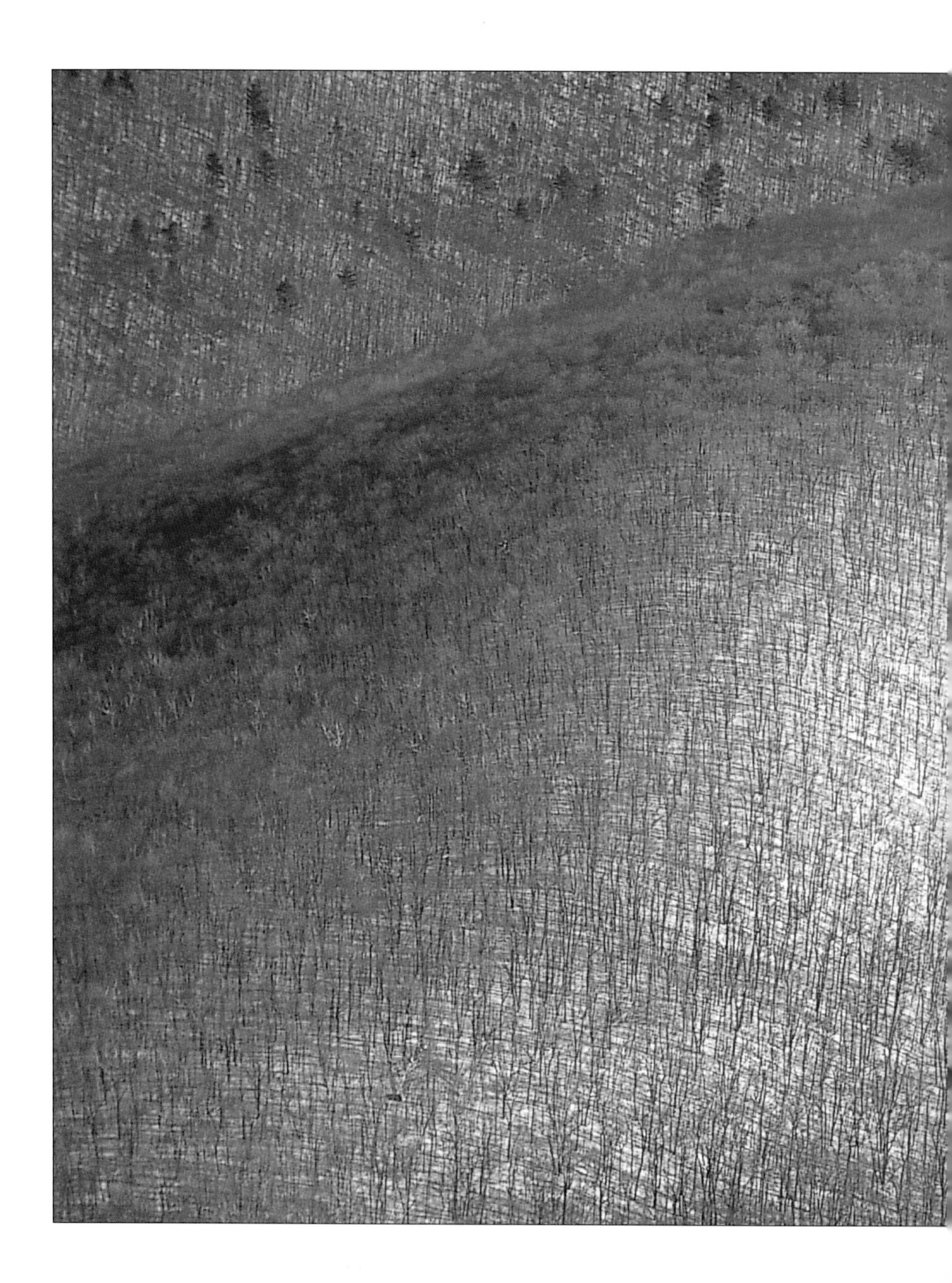

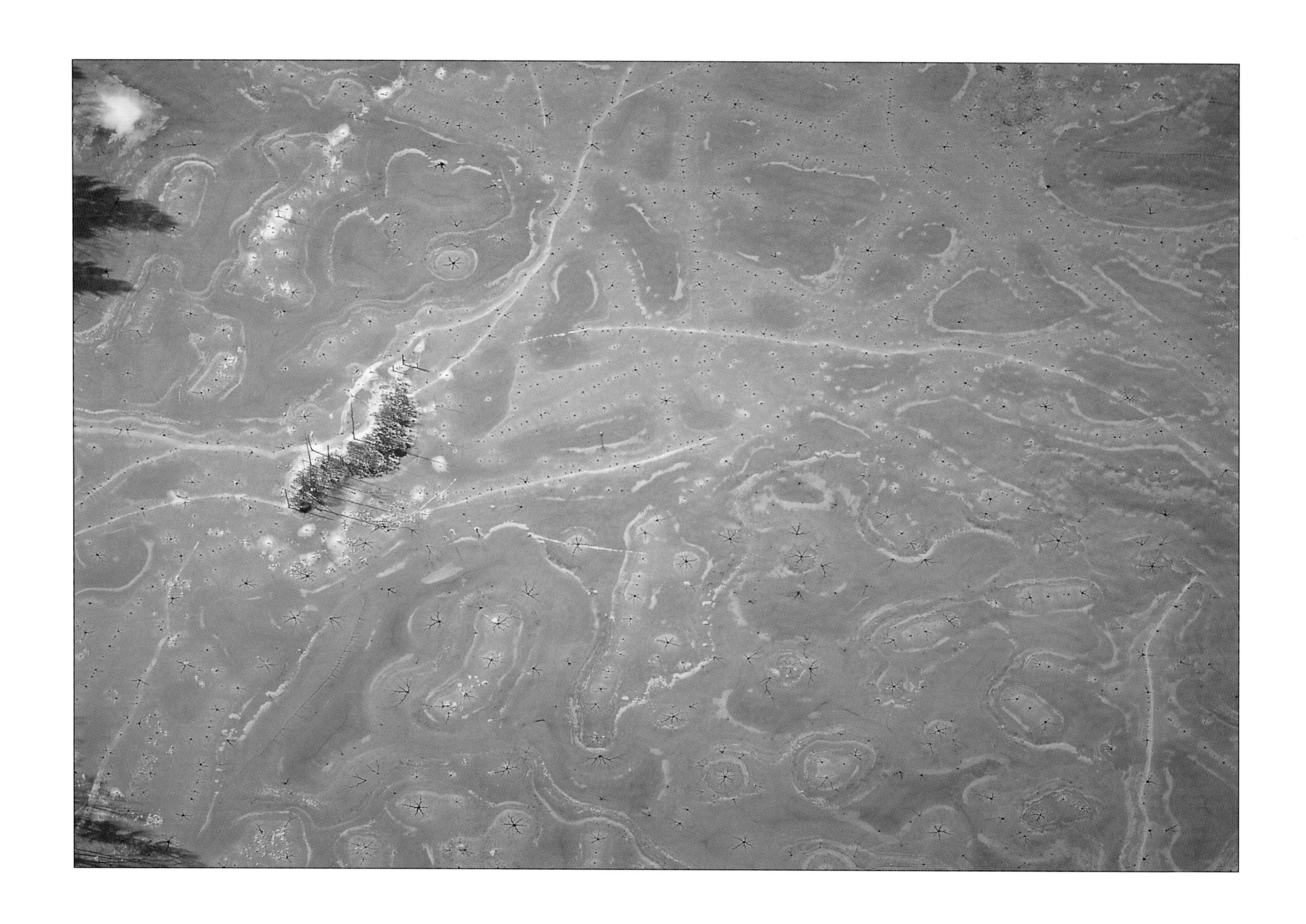

Constant melting and freezing created this abstract on a frozen lake in the western part of the state.

From the ground, the winter landscape may seem bleak and barren, but from my position aloft, I saw a never-ending variety of shapes and textures including these.

In winter, frozen lakes provide Mother Nature with an opportunity to exercise her artistic skills. This beaver-like imagine appeared on an icy canvas in western Massachusetts.

In life and in art,

the shortest distance between two points can be very dull. This is true whether you're flying a plane or scouting for a good camera shot—and especially if you're doing both at the same time. The paths between my photography and my flying wandered for some twenty years before finally connecting.

I first picked up a camera in the mid-sixties, while still in my teens. I had joined VISTA (the domestic Peace Corps) and lived in a barrio in Albuquerque, working with Mexican-Americans. When the first shadows of an image began to rise on the paper in the tray of developer, I knew I was onto something. From then on, I took a camera with me everywhere. Magazines and newspapers bought my photographs, and I went to Africa three times on assignment. But when I saw that most of my work was being done for corporations and for advertising, I moved to Maine and started an outerwear design business with my lifetime mate.

In January 1992, a friend asked to borrow a set of strobe lights. He was a flight instructor and offered to trade a few hours of training for the use of the lights. I accepted. Almost immediately, I had visions of marrying my photographic talent to my newfound love of flight. Less than two years later, after earning my instrument rating and then a commercial license, I began taking photos of the Maine countryside in earnest. Not long after that, I bought my first airplane and set it up for my particular style of making photographs.

I prefer to work with as few encumbrances as possible, so I don't use any steadying apparatus or special filters. My technique requires just my instincts, an open window, a 35mm Nikon camera, a couple of good lenses, Fujichrome slide film, and quick visual editing of an immense subject. My photographs are intended to be my own unique, spontaneous impressions of the landscape and all its textures.